Your Shadow Wants to Walk Alone

Dear Romi,
Best wishes,
[signature]
Dec 4 2015

Your Shadow Wants to Walk Alone

A book of Hindi-English poems

SANDEEP KISHORE

RUPA

Published by
Rupa Publications India Pvt. Ltd 2015
7/16, Ansari Road, Daryaganj
New Delhi 110002

Sales Centres:

Allahabad Bengaluru Chennai
Hyderabad Jaipur Kathmandu
Kolkata Mumbai

ISBN: 978-81-291-3691-6

Second impression 2015

10 9 8 7 6 5 4 3 2

The moral right of the author has been asserted.

Printed by Replika Press Pvt. Ltd, India

मोहब्बत हमने की लेकिन
निभाना तुमसे सीखा है

ये किताब
मेरी ज़िन्दगी और जीवनसाथी
सुशमा
के नाम

This book is dedicated to
my life and life partner
Sushma

for your courage, love and faith...

Contents

Prologue   *xiii*

1. कभी तो आओगे सनम   1
   Someday you will be here   3

2. पलकों पर रख कर जीते हैं   5
   You are in my soul   7

3. बदलाव   9
   The journey of change   11

4. कल का सूरज   13
   A new dawn   15

5. अक्सर बातें करते हैं   17
   I often talk to myself   19

6. चाँद   21
   The moon   23

7. पंख दिये अरमानों को   25
   Giving wings to aspirations   26

8. क्यों करें हम इंतज़ार   27
   Why should we wait   29

9. यादें   31
   Memories   33
10. बेटियाँ जल्द बड़ी हो जाती हैं   35
   Daughters grow up too fast   37
11. यहीं तो हो   39
   You are here   42
12. बारिश   44
   Rain   46
13. मुस्कुराहट   48
   Smile   49
14. मुलाकात   50
   Meeting   51
15. खालीपन   52
   Emptiness   54
16. बहते आँसू   56
   Tears   57
17. गुस्सा   58
   Anger   59
18. परदा   60
   Veil   61

19. सच-झूठ   62
Truth and lies   63

20. मुखड़ा   64
Face   65

21. परछाईं   66
Shadow   67

22. दिलजला   68
The burning heart   69

23. परिवर्तन   70
The change   71

24. शर्माना   72
Blush   73

25. रूठने का मज़ा   74
Pleasure of getting upset   75

26. जी चाहता है   76
I want to   78

27. धरोहर   80
Inheritance   82

28. ज़िन्दगी   85
Life   86

29. रूठना   87
   Upset   89

30. मुबारक   91
   Congratulations   93

31. आईना   95
   Mirror   96

32. कहानी   97
   Story   98

33. ज़िन्दगी अब भी प्यारी है   99
   Life is still beautiful   100

34. चार्ली चैपलिन को समर्पित   102
   Dedicated to Charlie Chaplin   103

35. ढूँढना   104
   To find   105

36. दोराहा   106
   Crossroads   107

Acknowledgements   109
Cause, Commitment and Support   113

Prologue

Emotions are like shadows; they are an integral part of our personality and make us who we are. What happens if we let our shadow create its own identity? What happens if we let the shadow walk alone? *Your Shadow Wants to Walk Alone* is about sentiments, aspirations, desires, hope, changes, expectations, pain, growing up, dreams, failures, successes and much more. It is about all of us.

Your Shadow Wants to Walk Alone is a book of poems. Originally written in Hindi, these poems have been translated by me into English to connect with one and all, within India and globally. Emotions are universal and they transcend all barriers of geography, age or race.

For me, writing poetry is about passionately capturing the imagination, thoughts, dreams and life itself through its various phases. All of these connect with one another, even though they appear disjointed many a time. They capture multiple shades. Some of them drive the simplicity of dreams and aspirations, while others contemplate a different way of thinking. Some reflect from deep within and some look far away. The canvas of life is massive and each shade is beautiful...depending on how it is seen.

I cannot recall exactly how old I was when I wrote my first poem in Hindi. I was often invited to recite them at family gatherings. Writing poetry gained momentum during my undergrad years at IIT Bombay, when I also edited the campus' Hindi magazine. I continued writing on and off after I started my career in India and then in the US. Over the years, I have written many poems, and only recently decided to give them a shape by publishing a selection in this book.

I hope these poems touch and connect with you. We go through multiple phases in life, and as you go through these poems, I hope they speak to you in your own flow and emotions.

Sandeep Kishore
May 2015

1. कभी तो आओगे सनम

महफ़िल में जो गये
उनके बिना थे हम
किस्सों में, कहानियों में
उनको कहा सनम

कुछ चेहरे उनके उभरने लगे
कुछ फ़साने सच लगने लगे

कहा हमने दिल से थाम ले तू
ख़्वाबों के पिटारों को
यूँ ही नहीं आते हैं
सपनों में बसने वाले

चलो चलें खींच लायें और उनकी यादों को
शायद कहीं उनको भी दर्द मेरा छू जाये
शायद उनके होठों पे
नाम मेरा आ जाये

या फिर देखें कब तक हमसे
वो भी रूठे रहते हैं
कब तक सपनों की गलियों में

वो भी हमसे छुपते हैं

हम आज भी उसी आँगन में बैठे हैं
जहाँ तुम्हारा आँचल
फिसल सा जाता था
जब भी हँसती थी तुम

उफ़, वो हँसी...

महफ़िल भी है, नग़मे भी
सपने भी हैं, क़िस्से भी
दर्पण भी है, चेहरे भी
उम्मीद भी, आरज़ू भी है

कभी तो आओगे सनम
कभी तो आओगे

1. Some day you will be here

I went to the party
and talked about her as my sweetheart
in tales and stories,
her face started to appear
and dreams seemed to be coming true.

I said to my heart,
hold on to the fantasies,
one who lives in our dream
doesn't come by so easily.

Let's draw
her memories together,
perhaps my pain will call her
perhaps my name will come to her lips.

Or let's see how long
she remains elusive,
for how long she continues to

hide in my dreams.

Even now, I sit
in the same verandah
where her scarf would slip,
every time she laughed.

Oh, that laughter!

People are there
so are the poems,
dreams are there
so are the stories,
mirrors are there
so are the faces,
expectations are there,
desires too.

Sweetheart
some day you will be here,
I know, you will be.

2. पलकों पर रख कर जीते हैं

मैं क्या कहूँ तुमसे सनम
हर रोज़ तुम्हारी यादों को
पलकों पर रख कर जीते हैं
पलकों पर रख कर जीते हैं

वो मखमली चेहरा तेरा
लगता है छू कर चला गया
वो मीठी मीठी हँसी तुम्हारी
अभी यहीं पर रुकी हुई है

वो दबे पाँव आना तेरा
चुपके से मुझको चौंका देना
फिर हंसना इतनी ज़ोरों से
एक रोज़ हमारी जान लेगा

लब सिले हुए से लगते हैं
कितने क़िस्से कह जाते हैं
उन प्यासे नयनों से पूछो
जो राह तुम्हारी तकते हैं

चुपचाप तुम्हारी आँखो में
मैं खोजा करता अक्सर हूँ
अपने जीवन की परिभाषा
मैंने देखी है अपनों में

मैं क्या कहूँ तुमसे सनम
हर रोज़ तुम्हारी यादों को
पलकों पर रख कर जीते हैं
पलकों पर रख कर जीते हैं

2. *You are in my soul*

What can I tell you,
everyday I live
I live with your memories in my soul.

It feels like your angelic face
has just touched me and moved away,
but your sweet smile
still lingers on.

Your mischievous steps
catch me with total surprise,
and your hearty laughter
will take my life away one day.

Your sealed lips
tell so many tales,
ask my thirsty eyes
that look for your sight.

What I silently
search for in your eyes,
the meaning of our lives
I find deep within ourselves.
What can I tell you,
everyday I live
I live with your memories in my soul.

3. बदलाव

उम्मीद के दरिया में
हम बहते चले गये
अच्छा हुआ किसी ने भी
जो हाथ न थामा

मुड़ते ही निगाहें फेर ली
अपनों ने भी हमसे
चुपचाप रास्ते पर
मैं अकेला ही चलता रहा

किस-किस को याद करूँ
किस-किस पर जान दूँ
अपनी ही ज़िद थी
एक नयी राह की

उड़ने की चाह मन में
घर जो कर गयी
पंख का भी हमें तो
इंतज़ार ना हुआ

घायल हुआ शरीर
मन फिर भी बुलंद था
नये सूरज की राह में
हमें जलना कूबूल था

उठेगी ज़िन्दगी नयी
नये अरमाँ सजायेगी
बदलाव की डगर
नया रंग तो लायेगी
नया रंग तो लायेगी

3. The journey of change

I travelled on
the sea of hope,
it was just as well
no one took my hand.

All those I considered mine
turned away from me,
silently I left on my own
on this journey.

Who should I remember
who should I give my life for,
it was my own resolve
to find a new way.

The desire to fly
took hold of me so intensely,
I couldn't even wait
for the wings to grow.

The body was bruised
yet, the mind was enthused
I was willing to burn
to discover the new sun.

New life will rise again
bringing with it new hope,
the journey of change
will certainly bring new hues.
It will.

4. कल का सूरज

बड़ी उम्मीद है सबको
बड़ी मेहनत से सींचा है
ज़माना साथ आगे है
दुआ जो उठ रही देखो

बदलते बादलों के रंग
हवा के रूख में तेज़ी है
पुकारें गूँज बन गयी
लहू गरम भी हो रहा

जोशे जूनून का आलम है
शंखनाद है चारों ओर
बुलंद इरादे हैं सब के
बदल डालें अब कल को

कल जब सूरज निकलेगा
किरणें जो उसकी बिखरेंगी
वो नई रोशनी, नई सुबह
दिशाएं नई, अरमान नए

कल के सूरज में, कुछ नई मस्ती भी होगी
जवाबदेही का एहसास भी
कुछ नया करने की हसरत भी होगी
सब को साथ ले कर चलना भी होगा

बीते कल से, कुछ सीखना तो होगा
और नये विचारों को लाना भी होगा
एक नया कल बनाना ज़रूरी है
नये सूरज का आना ज़रूरी है

4. A new dawn

Everyone has high hopes
everyone has worked hard for it,
the whole world is coming together
look at the prayers that are rising.

The clouds are changing colour
and the winds are blowing hard,
calls have reached a crescendo
and the mercury is rising fast.

Adrenaline rush is there
trumpets blowing everywhere,
all are determined
to change tomorrow.

As the sun rises tomorrow
it will bring new light,
a new day
new directions and new aspirations.

Tomorrow's sun will have new excitement
and also have a sense of responsibility,
the desire to do something new will be there
so will the need to keep everyone together.

We must learn from the past
and also bring new thoughts for the future,
it's important to make a new tomorrow
it's a must to have a new dawn.

5. अक्सर बातें करते हैं

कभी सुनाते हैं ख़ुद को
कभी सुनते भी हैं ख़ुद की
ढूंढ के लाते हैं समय को
ख़ुद से बातें करने को

जीतना होगा इस बार हमें
चाहे कितनी भी अड़चनें हों
जूझना होगा हर बार हमें
करनी होगी मुश्किल आसान

इसको ऐसे करना था
उसको वैसे कहना था
कुछ और करो अभ्यास अभी
तैयारी थोड़ी कच्ची है

मन कहता रहता है हमसे
बेहतर बनने की आदत
ज़ेहन में डालनी पड़ती है
ख़ुद को ख़ुद की लड़ाई
अक्सर लड़नी पड़ती है

कुछ करने की हिम्मत हो
कुछ कहने की हसरत हो
ख़ुद को हमेशा सुना करो
ख़ुद से हमेशा कहा करो

हर बार अकेले में यूँ ही
हम अक्सर बातें करते हैं
हर बार अकेले में यूँ ही
हम अक्सर बातें करते हैं

5. I often talk to myself

I often find time
to talk to myself.

I have to succeed this time
no matter how many obstacles come,
I have to fight all the time
to make them easier.

It should have been done like this
it should have been said like that,
Let's practice some more
preparation is still inadequate.

The mind says all the time
internalize the habit to get better,
more often
it's a struggle with one's self.

Have the courage to do

the desire to speak,
always listen to yourself
always speak with yourself.

Whenever I am alone,
I often talk to myself.
Whenever I am alone
I often talk to myself.

6. चाँद

उस दिन जो हमने
पकड़ लिया
अपनी मुट्ठी में चाँद
लगा जैसे
अरसों से किया है चाँद ने इंतज़ार

सिमट कर हाथ में आया
कहा, काफ़ी देर लगा दी

मैं देखा करता हूँ रोज़ाना
निहारें सब मेरी ओर
मनसूबे भी कई करते हैं
हिम्मत तो है अनेकों की

उछल कर पकड़ने की है ज़रूरत
मैं जान बूझ कर हूँ इतनी दूर

मैं क्यों आकार बदलता हूँ
खेलूँ सूरज की किरणों से
कभी पूरा हूँ, कभी आधा
कभी-कभी तो हो कर भी
उसके पीछे छुप जाता हूँ

जिन्हें ढूँढने की है हसरत
वो रूकते नहीं हैं रात को
पूर्णिमा हो, या हो अमावस
उनके अन्दर की रोशनी
मैंने देखी है जलते हमेशा

मुश्किल तो है, नामुमकिन नहीं
करता हूँ मैं भी इंतज़ार
जाओ पकड़ो अपने चाँद को
जाओ पकड़ो अपने चाँद को

6. The moon

The day I took
the moon in my hand
it looked,
as if it had been waiting
for me, for a very long time.

It settled
in my hand
and said,
you took a while.

I observe them everyday
everyone looks at me
many desire me
but a few have the courage
to grab me.

All it takes is to jump
and get me,
I am far

for a reason.

I play with the sun's rays
and change my shape,
sometimes, I am complete
and sometimes half,
I even hide behind the sun
to get away.

People with deep conviction
don't rest at night,
be it a full
or
moonless night.

I always see their
inner light to be on.

It's difficult, but not impossible...
Even I wait.

Go and get your own moon.
Go and get your own moon.

7. पंख दिये अरमानों को

पंख दिये अरमानों को
उड़ने की चाहत सब को दी
उम्मीद जगाने की हसरत
आदत सी बनती देखी है

कितनी भी मुश्किल डगर
जादू का आलम हरदम है
सतरंगी सपने बादल से
बुनने की आदत सीखी है

एक रास्ते सी ज़िंदगी
हर मोड़ नया आयाम है
नये सपने, दिशाएँ, उम्मीदें
हौसला वही, कुछ नया करने की चाहत वही

7. Giving wings to aspirations

Giving wings to aspirations
the will to fly,
desire to believe in hope
I have seen it become a habit.

No matter how difficult the roads are
the magic is always in the air,
have learned the habit to weave
rainbows from the cloud.

Life is a journey
every turn is a new dimension,
new dreams, directions, expectations
the same courage and the desire to do something new.

8. क्यों करें हम इंतज़ार

कहीं जो दूर बैठे हैं
कभी गुमसुम से लगते हैं
निगाहें फेरने की भी
अदा तो नहीं आती

वो जो आयेंगे, तो हम
ये भी जान जायेंगे
की मोहब्बत हमसे ज़्यादा है
या ज़िद उनको प्यारी है

पकड़ूँ उनकी साँसों को
या खेलूँ उनके दामन से
अपने तनहा मन को तो
हमने है कहना छोड़ दिया

हर रोज़ उनकी आँखें भी
कुछ बातें यूँ कर जाती हैं
जैसे धड़कनों ने उड़ कर
अपनी ख़ुशबू बिखरायी है

किसकी ज़िद है, किसका गुस्सा
साँसें, दामन, आँखे, बातें
धड़कन, ख़ुशबू, तनहा मोहब्बत

क्यों करें हम इंतज़ार
क्यों करें हम इंतज़ार

8. Why should we wait

Sitting far away
at times, she looks lost
still not able to,
take her eyes away from me.

When she will walk towards me
I will know,
if she loves me more
or wants to remain stubborn.

Should I capture her breath
or play with her stole,
I have stopped asking
my lonely mind.

Her eyes tell
so many tales everyday,
as the heartbeat has fluttered
and spread as a beautiful fragrance.

Whose whim and whose anger is this.
Breath, stole, eyes, tales
heartbeat, fragrance, solitary love.

Why should we wait,
why should we wait.

9. यादें

भूलना तुमको आता है
यादें मुझको प्यारी हैं

जब रातें कटती हैं आँखो में
और नींद समुंदर होता है
चुपचाप हमारे ख़्वाबों में
तुम धीरे से आ जाती हो

हम पूछते रहते हैं तुमसे
तुम गुमसुम हमेशा रहती हो
साँसें, धड़कन, चाहत मेरी
नज़रें तुम्हारी, जीवन मेरा

तुम्हारे आने की ख़ुशबू भी
रंग हज़ार सजाएगी
वो लम्हा ठहर सा जायेगा
कुछ कहना नहीं, कुछ सुनना नहीं

जब आँखे दर्पण बनती हैं
वो दिल की बात समझती हैं
क़दमों की आहट से भी हम
उम्मीद जगाया करते हैं

हवा जो मद्धम हो गयी
शायद इंतज़ार उसको भी है

ऐ रब, अब तो मुझे बता
क्या कहूँ, किससे कहूँ
कब कहूँ, कितना कहूँ

हमने अपने को सनम
आप ही में देखा है
हमने अपने को सनम
आप ही में देखा है

9. Memories

You seem to forget,
I love to remember.

With sleep as deep as ocean
you slowly appear in my dreams.

I ask you
but you are so quiet,
my breath, heartbeat, love
your eyes and my life.

The aroma of your arrival
will spread a thousand colours,
the moment will pause
nothing to say
nothing to hear.

When eyes reflect the soul
they know what the heart says,
I raise my hope

from the sound of every footstep I hear.

Look, even the wind is calm
perhaps, it also awaits your arrival.

O God,
What should I tell and to whom.
When should I tell and how much.

I see myself in you.
I do.

10. बेटियाँ जल्द बड़ी हो जाती हैं

एक प्यारी नन्ही परी जैसी
उड़ कर मेरी गोद में
महसूस अभी भी होता है
बेटियाँ इतनी जल्द क्यों बड़ी हो जाती हैं

वो पहला शब्द, जो सुनने की
हर दिन होती थी आरज़ू हमारी
सुनने की इतनी अभिलाषा
बेटियाँ इतनी जल्द क्यों बड़ी हो जाती हैं

किसी तरह से गिरते-पड़ते भी
जब चार कदम सीधी चली
वो ख़ुशी कैसे भूल सकेंगे
बेटियाँ इतनी जल्द क्यों बड़ी हो जाती हैं

एक खूबसूरत कल
बाँहें खोले करे इन्तज़ार
अरमानों के पंख लगा कर
उड़ कर उसे ढूँढना है

राहें आसान हों या मुश्किल
हर मोड़ नया आयाम है
हौसले हों बुलंद हमेशा
दिशायें सामने आ जायेंगी

ख़ुद पर विश्वास हमेशा हो
कभी गिरना है, तो उठना भी
कभी चलना है, कभी उड़ना भी
सितारे भी तो लाने हैं, मंज़िलें ख़ुद बनानी हैं

जिस ख़ूबसूरत मोड़ पर है ज़िंदगी पहुँच गई
जाओ, एक और भी सुनहरा कल बनाओ
बेटियाँ जल्द बड़ी हो जाती हैं
बेटियाँ जल्द बड़ी हो जाती हैं

10. Daughters grow up too fast

Like a beautiful little fairy
you flew straight into my lap
oh, I can still feel it.
Why do daughters grow up so fast.

I craved for
that first word every day,
such anticipation to hear.
Why do daughters grow up so fast.

I remember the first few steps
when you somehow walked straight,
I can never forget that joy.
Why do daughters grow up so fast.

A beautiful tomorrow
awaits with open arms,
you have to fly with the wings of aspirations
to discover it.

The roads may be rough or easy
but every turn is a new opportunity,
with courage and strong determination
directions will reveal themselves.

Always believe in yourself
if you fall, you must get up
sometimes you walk
and sometimes fly.

You must reach for the stars
and make your own destiny,
life has reached a beautiful turn for you
go and make it an even better tomorrow.

Daughters do grow up fast,
they do.

11. यहीं तो हो

इन दिनों
देख रहा हूँ
महसूस भी
कर रहा हूँ
परेशाँ मन
खोजता
रहता है
पता है उसे
तुम,
कहीं तो होगी

बेचैन सी
आवाज़
ढूँढता है
हर तरफ़
हल्की सी
आहट
और
पलट कर
देखना,
शायद...

बंद दरवाज़े
वैसे ही हैं
जैसे कि तुम
छोड़ गयी थी,
अधखुली
खिड़कियों
को
लगता है
तुम आओगी
ज़रूर

हवा का
एक झोंका
तुम्हारी ख़ुशबू
ले कर
घूम आया है,
रहना तो उसे
मेरे पास ही है

न तुमसे करूँ
या न सोचूँ
तुम्हारी बात
तो
लगता है
जैसे कुछ
छूट सा रहा है

तुम हो
यहीं तो हो,
तुम हो
यहीं तो हो

11. *You are here*

These days
I see and feel it,
my pained mind
looks for you
knowing
you are
here,
somewhere.

Restless,
it searches for
your voice
everywhere,
a bit of sound
and it turns to see,
perhaps...

The door
is closed
as you had left them,

half-open windows
are hopeful
that you will
certainly be back.

Fragrance filled
whiff of air
has come back
after a round,
it knows, it has to stay
with me only.

If I don't
talk
or
think
about you,
it feels like
I am
losing something.

Surely, you are here
certainly here.

12. बारिश

दिन कितने भी बीतेंगे
मौसम आ कर जायेंगे
एहसास जैसे अब भी तुम
वहीं खड़ी हो बारिश में

हल्की बारिश की बूँदें
गिरने दो तुम चेहरे पर
सौंधी सी जो ख़ुशबू है
आने दो इन साँसों में

गिरती बूँदें खिलता चेहरा
बाँहें खुली और आँखें बंद
फिसलने का डर भी नहीं
गोल-गोल सा घूमना

बेपरवाह सी सड़क पर
लाज किसी से आये क्यों
होंठों पर गीतों का आना
फिर मुझे खींचना बारिश में

जब-जब बारिश आती है
बूँदों में दिखती तुम ही तुम
अल्हड़ सी वो हँसी तुम्हारी
जादू सा कर जाती है

चलो बारिश में फिर भीगें हम
चलो बारिश में फिर भीगें हम

12. *Rain*

Days will come and go
seasons will change,
feels like you are still
standing in the rain.

Let the drops of rain
fall on your face,
let the aroma of wet earth
fill your breath.

Falling raindrops, smiling face
open arms and closed eyes,
you are never scared of slipping
while dancing in the rain.

You are not shy
on the careless road,
songs come to your lips
and you pull me in the rain.

Every time the rain comes
I see you in the raindrops,
your carefree laughter
creates the magic.

Come let's get wet in the rain again.
Come let's get wet in the rain again.

13. मुस्कुराहट

यूँ तो कोई
शिकायत नहीं तुमसे
पर उदास होते हो तुम
तो अच्छा नहीं लगता

ज़िन्दगी के हर पहलू से
परेशाँ हो चुका हूँ मैं
एक तेरी मुस्कुराहट का
आसरा ही तो है

13. Smile

I don't have any
complaints of you,
but I don't feel right
when you are sad.

I am overwhelmed
with everything else in life,
It's only your smile
that keeps me going.

14. मुलाकात

वो तो किस्मत थी मेरी
जो आपसे मुलाकात हुई
वरना इस महफ़िल में हमें
पूछता ही कौन था

14. *Meeting*

It was my great fortune
that I met with you,
otherwise who would have
bothered about me in this gathering.

15. ख़ालीपन

बवंडर से उठते
विचारों के साये में
चुपचाप बैठा था
कमरे के बाहर

ख़यालों में था कि
किसे रूप दूँ मैं
किसे जिस्म दूँ मैं
किसे जान दूँ मैं

बस इतने में
तूफ़ानी आँधी की तरह
झंझोरा किसी ने
तो सपने भी टूटे
विचारों की श्रृंखला
अधूरी ही रह गयी

बड़े अनमनेपन से पूछा
क्या है
दिखता नहीं, मैं सोच रहा हूँ
अरे, सोचना कैसे दिखता है यार

अनायास ही हँस पड़ा था मैं
कुछ उसके जवाब पर
कुछ अपनी झुँझलाहट पर

आजकल अजीब सी ख़ामोशी है
अजीब सा सन्नाटा है
इसमें उठते हुए
विचारों को
पकड़ नहीं पा रहा हूँ मैं

आज तीसरा दिन है
मैं चुपचाप बैठा हूँ
कमरे के बाहर
कलम हाथ में है
दिमाग़ है ख़ाली
और निहार रहा हूँ
उस अनंत आकाश को
जिसकी गोद में
'लाल' सा सूरज
सोने जा रहा है
थक कर

15. *Emptiness*

I was outside the room
amidst various thoughts,
and wondered
what to write.

Suddenly someone
shook me up,
and all my thoughts
went away.

I asked,
with sheer disappointment
what is this,
Can't you see I am thinking.

Oh,
how do you see thinking,
I laughed
a little at his answer
and a little at my disenchantment.

The days are
calm and quiet,
strange
and unique.

It's the third day today
I am still outside the room,
I have the pen
but no thoughts

and,
I am observing the infinite sky
that is embracing the red sun
within its horizon,
like a mother who
takes her tired baby
into her arms to sleep.

16. बहते आँसू

कोई रखे अरसों तक
और कोई निकाले पल भर में
आँखो से आँसू गिरने में
कोई दर्द तो होता है

फिसलती रेत, मुट्ठियों से
यूँ गिर ही जाती है
जो आँखो में आते हैं आँसू
वो वापस फिर नहीं जाते

उनकी भाषा भी अद्भुत है
जो चुप रह कर
अपनी बातें
किस मर्म से कह जाते हैं

सही ग़लत की बात नहीं
समझो हमको, ये कहते हैं
शायद, इसीलिये बहते हैं
शायद, इसीलिये बहते हैं

16. Tears

Some hold them back for ages
and some let them fall fast,
but whenever a tear falls
an ache twists somewhere.

Fleeting sand always slips
through the fingers,
and the tears that come to the eyes
never go back.

Their language is strange
that in their silence,
they always communicate
the pain.

It's not about right or wrong
they say, please try to understand.
Perhaps, that's why tears fall,
perhaps, that's why tears fall.

17. गुस्सा

ख़ुद करो रोज़ गुस्सा
तो ये अदा है तुम्हारी
कभी जो ख़फ़ा हैं हम
तो नाराज़ हो गये

17. *Anger*

When you get angry with me everyday
you call it your style,
then when I am annoyed even for a day
why do you get upset.

18. परदा

सब ने देखा तुम्हें
सब ने आहें भरीं
हम जो महफ़िल में आए
तो हमसे परदा है क्यों

18. Veil

Everyone saw you
and everyone sighed,
when I arrived at the gathering
why did you put on your veil.

19. सच-झूठ

मीठी लगी मुझे वो बात
पर, नफ़रत है मुझे झूठ के
हर एक फ़साने से

सच सुनने की भी तो
मुझे हिम्मत नहीं होती

ऐ रब, मुझे एक रोज़
तो तू हौसला यूँ दे
कह तो सकूँ, मैं दिल से
कि यूँ ही बहल रहा है तू

19. Truth and lies

I heard the sweet talk
but, I hate tales of lies.

How do I gather the strength
to hear the truth.

O God, one day
give me the courage
to tell my heart,
it is entertained by delusion.

20. मुखड़ा

एक पल जो देखा आपको
कुर्बान हो गया
मैं यूँ ही मर गया होता
गर भर नज़र जो देख लेता

20. Face

I glanced at you
and fell head over heels,
I would have died just like that
if I had seen you a bit longer.

21. परछाई

जब रोशनी थी साथ में
तो तुम भी साथ थे मेरे
अंधेरा जो मिला मुझे
तो जाने कहाँ खो गये

हैरान हूँ
क्या सीखूँ
आत्म निर्भरता
या
बेवफ़ाई

21. Shadow

When there was light
you were by my side,
when I encountered darkness
you left me alone.

I wonder,
what to learn
self-reliance
or
betrayal.

22. दिलजला

रातों को हौले-हौले
हमने सुनाई दिल को
वो दास्ताँ हमने
वापस सुनाई दिल को

हसरत ने ज़िन्दा रखा
हसरतों ने ही मारा
जब-जब हुआ अंधेरा
हमने जलाया दिल को

22. The burning heart

Slowly and steadily
giving comfort to the heart,
the story gets told
many times over.

A desire keeps me alive
and many of them kill me,
when there is darkness
my heart burns to light the life.

23. परिवर्तन

वो मुस्कुराहट जो उनकी थी
है बदली-बदली सी, तो क्या

वो शरमाती जो आँखें थी
हैं ओझल-ओझल सी, तो क्या

वो बेताबी जो नज़रों में थी
ग़ायब हो गयी, तो क्या

बढ़ी धड़कन जो रहती थी
धीमी हो गयी, तो क्या

मोहब्बत में लोगों का
तो कुछ भी हाल होता है

ख़ुशबू जो रहती थी साँसों में
यादें जो बसी थीं ख़्वाबों में
टिप-टिप कर के बूँदों सी
हैं बरस रही इन आँखों से

23. The change

So what if her
smile has changed.

So what if her shy eyes
are now concealed.

So what if her look of
eagerness has vanished.

So what if her
heartbeat is now calm.

People in love
do behave differently.

The fragrance of her breath
and the dreams of her memories,
find expression through the eyes
as tears of love.

24. शर्माना

वो नयन उनके अधखुले से
खुलते धीरे-धीरे थे

वो मुखड़ा उनका धीरे से जब
मंद-मंद मुस्काता था

होंठों पे धीरे-धीरे से जब
बात प्यार की आती थी

जब चंचल सी उनकी नज़रें
यूँ मुझसे टकरा जाती थी
सच बात कहूँ, ऐ दिल मेरे
वो यूँ ही शर्मा जाती थी

24. Blush

Her half-open eyes
would open slowly.

The smile on her face
would slowly emerge.

Her lips would slowly
whisper words of love.

When her playful eyes
would catch mine

O my heart!

To tell you the truth,
she would simply blush.

25. रूठने का मज़ा

रूठने का मज़ा
तभी है सनम
जब कोई देखे
और मनाए भी

25. Pleasure of getting upset

The pleasure of getting upset
is only there
when someone cares
and persudes too.

26. जी चाहता है

जब भी देखूँ तुम्हारी तरफ़
दिल से मुस्कुराने को जी चाहता है

ज़माने से होकर परेशाँ जो निकले
तेरे चौखट पे आने को जी चाहता है

कब तक यूँ ही भटकते रहेंगे
तेरा दामन थामने को जी चाहता है

तुमको खोया है हमने न जाने कहाँ पर
हर तरफ ढूँढने को जी चाहता है

सम्भालो हमें हम तो गिरने लगे हैं
तुमसे गले मिलने को जी चाहता है

मोहब्बत करने को जी चाहता है
ज़िन्दगी जीने को जी चाहता है

एक बार तो देखो इस तरफ़
फिर से मुस्कुराने को जी चाहता है

जब भी देखूँ तुम्हारी तरफ़
दिल से मुस्कुराने को जी चाहता है

26. I want to

Whenever I look at you
I want to smile so much.

Stressed with the world
I want to come to your door.

For how long will I keep wandering,
I want to be with you.

Don't know where did I lose you
I look for you everywhere.

Hold me, as I am going to fall
I want to be in your arms.

I want to fall in love
I want to live.

Look at me just once
I want to smile again.

Whenever I look at you
I want to smile so much.

27. धरोहर

एक रोज़ मुझको रास्ते में
मिल गयी थी ज़िन्दगी
इससे पहले मैं कुछ पूछूँ
पूछ बैठी ज़िन्दगी

हमने जब भी देखा है तुमको
खिले-खिले से रहते हो
जब हँसी तुम्हारे होठों पर
यूँ चुपके से आ जाती है

जब उम्मीदों के दामन पर
तुम उड़े-उड़े से रहते हो
सारे नग़मे जीवन के
जब गीत सुनाया करते हैं

जो याद बहुत ही आते हैं
कब उनसे मिलने जाओगे

माँ की ममता भरी गोद में
जब हम ग़म सारे भूला करते थे
सही नसीहत पापा से

नई उम्मीद जगाया करती थी

भाईयों की छोटी-छोटी खिटपिट में
अपनेपन का एहसास हमेशा रहता था
वो बदमाशियाँ जो हमने की
और नानी-दादी ने साथ दिया

ये हँसी तुम्हारे जीवन की
कईयों ने बाँटी है खुशबू
कुछ हैं यहीं, कुछ चले गये
हर एक ने अपने से बढ़कर
माना था तुमको जीवन में

जीवन की आपा-धापी में
तुम भूल गये हो कुछ बातें
जो मिली तुम्हे धरोहर है
उसे रखना नहीं है अपने पास

जो कुछ है पाया अपनों से
उसे यहीं पर बाँट चलो
एक और ज़माना उठ रहा है
जिन्हें ज़रूरत है इनकी
ममता, प्यार, हँसी, नसीहत, विश्वास
और अपनापन, अपनापन, अपनापन

27. Inheritance

Once on a journey, I met with life
before I could, life asked me.

Whenever I see you
you always seem happy,
the smile on your lips
comes so naturally.

When you keep flying high
with ambitions and desires,
when all the songs of life
play melodies for you.

For those
who you remember so dearly,
when will you find time to meet.

All the sorrows would disappear

in the affectionate shade of my mother,
right advice from my father
would bring new hope.

The squabbles and fights with my brothers
always had a sense of belonging,
and how we got away from all the mischiefs we did
with compassionate support from our grandmothers.

The laughter in your life
to which many have added
some are here and some are not,
everyone loved you
more than themselves.

In the intensity of life
you forgot a few things,
the inheritance you have
is not for you to keep.

Whatever you have of your own
must be distributed here itself,
a new generation is here
that needs
affection, love, laughter, advice, trust
and
togetherness.

28. ज़िन्दगी

हसरतों के बहकावों ने
फैलाया अपना दामन इतना
कि एक आयाम में देखोगे
तो कुछ भी नहीं पाओगे

ज़िन्दगी एक प्रतिबिम्ब नहीं
जो सिमट कर सामने आ जाये
क़रीब जब तुम जाओगे
एहसास तब ही पाओगे

28. Life

Desires have spread
themselves so vast,
that one frame
cannot capture enough.

Life is not a shadow
that will shrink and come together at once,
Only when you live it closely
will you know it deep within.

29. रूठना

बड़ा ज़िद्दी है वो
जब रूठा होता है
तब बात तक नहीं करता
घंटों इंतज़ार करवाता है
पास तक नहीं आने देता

उसे मेरी ये दशा
ज़्यादा देर तक
अच्छी भी नहीं लगती
शायद, इसलिए
मान भी जाता है

सोचता हूँ
मैं भी तो यही करता था
जब छोटा था
मेरी माँ खाना भी नहीं खाती थी
जब मैं रूठा होता था

फिर, मैं जाता था
उनके पास, उनको मनाने
और, अपनी ज़िद भूल जाता था

कुछ आदतें, कितनी आसानी से
अपने को अरसे तक क़ायम रखती हैं
समय के साथ नहीं बदलतीं वों

29. Upset

He is so stubborn
that he won't even talk to me
when he is upset,
I have to wait for hours
before he even
lets me come close.

He doesn't like me
to stay away from him, for so long
so agrees to become
my friend again.

I used to do the same
when I was a child,
my mother wouldn't even eat
till the time I was upset.

Then, I would go to her
to make it up,
and would forget

I was the one who was upset.

Some habits
are ingrained in us deep
they don't change with time.

30. मुबारक

महफिल में हम जो आए हैं
दुआएँ साथ लायें हैं
मन्नतों का मौसम है
ख़ुशियाँ ढेर सारी हों

चेहरे जो खिले-खिले से हैं
मोहब्बत इनकी आँखो में
कुछ लम्हें ठहर गए से हैं
वो ख़ूबसूरत दुल्हन है
और शहज़ादे भी ख़ूब जचें

नयनों से बातें होती हैं
मुखड़ा तो दिल का दर्पण है
ख़ूबसूरत बहार है चारों ओर
मस्ती के आलम में झूमें

धीमी-धीमी हँसी में देखो
कितनी यादें जुड़ी हुई हैं

सपनों से भी सुंदर जीवन हो
अरमानों के बाग़ों में
सारी उम्मीदें पूरी हों

ख़ुशियों से भरा संसार हमेशा
यूँ ही खिलता रहे तुम्हारा
यूँ ही खिलता रहे तुम्हारा

30. Congratulations

We have brought our blessings
to the ceremony,
it's the season of wishes
let there be happiness all around.

Their faces are shining bright
can see love in their eyes,
some moments stand still
she is a beautiful bride
and he is a charming prince.

Their eyes speak
faces show the feelings,
beautiful flowers are all around
it's a fun atmosphere to cherish.

Their gentle smiles
hide so many memories.

We wish you both a life
even more beautiful than dreams,
in the garden of aspirations,
May all your wishes be fulfilled.

May your world be full of happiness
and, may it always shine bright.

31. आईना

अब तो आइने से भी मेरी
हटती नहीं नज़र
जब से सूरत पे अपनी
तेरा चेहरा नज़र आने लगा

31. Mirror

I can't stop but
keep staring at the mirror,
ever since all I see
is your face in mine.

32. कहानी

हर एक की होती है
कहानी अपनी-अपनी

कुछ बोलतीं हैं

और,

कुछ को
ख़ुद समझना पड़ता है

32. *Story*

Everyone has
their own story.

Some speak out

and,

for others

you have to
understand them
yourself.

33. ज़िन्दगी अब भी प्यारी है

कभी जो मिली नहीं मंज़िल
जब राहें कभी ख़त्म ना हो
अंधेरे में जो चलना हो
मिल के भी ना मिलना हो

जब सूरज की सारी किरणें
टेढ़ी लगने लगती हैं
जब कोशिश पूरी कर के भी
परिणाम हासिल नहीं होता

ज़िन्दगी को विश्वास से
तब भी जीना पड़ता है
चाहे कितना भी दर्द हो
दर्द सहना ही पड़ता है

जब तक धड़कन है दिल में
और एक साँस भी बाक़ी है
उम्मीदों को छोड़ो क्यों

ज़िन्दगी अब भी प्यारी है
ज़िन्दगी अब भी प्यारी है

33. *Life is still beautiful*

When you don't find the destination
and the roads seem endless,
when you have to walk in the dark
and after you get what you want
it does not feel real.

When rays from the sun
appear twisted,
and you don't see the results
in spite of giving it all that you have.

You still have to live life
with faith,
you have to endure the pain
no matter how hard it gets.

For as long as
the heart beats
and,
even with the last breath remaining
why should you leave hope.

Life is still beautiful.
Life is still beautiful.

34. चार्ली चैपलिन को समर्पित

दिल के दर्द का पता
लबों को क्यूँ दें
वो तो औरों की
ख़ुशी के लिये हैं बनें

34. Dedicated to Charlie Chaplin

Why should I let my lips know
about the pain of my heart,
they are made
for the happiness of others.

35. ढूँढना

जो ढूँढोगे हमें प्यार से
तो हम मिल ही जाएगें
ये दिल इतना पागल है
कहीं और जाता ही नहीं

35. To find

If you look for me with love
you will always find me,
I love you so much
that I am always around.

36. दोराहा

हर बार
दोराहे पर

फिर वही
सवाल आया

और

हर बार की तरह
इस बार भी
दूसरा रास्ता
फिर से चुना

36. Crossroads

As always,
same question
came at
the crossroads

and,

as always
I took
the
alternate path.

Acknowledgements

Writing a few poems in isolation over the years is one thing, making a book from them is quite another. I realized this soon after I decided to publish this book. It is then that I found that the process of publishing a book takes a lot more than I had thought.

I have thoroughly enjoyed every step of this fascinating journey and am deeply honoured to be able to put this in front of all of you. Along this journey, I was fortunate to get some amazing help, support and insight from my family, friends, mentors and colleagues.

This book belongs as much to each of them, as it does to me. I am forever indebted to each and every one who has helped me in this journey.

My parents Asha Singh and Dr H.K. Singh have been the most important influences in my life. They have been a continuous source of love, affection and learning. Thank you very much Ma and Papa for your continuous support and encouragement.

Thanks to my awesome brothers and their families for their valuable inputs on the book—Prateek, Sangeeta, Pratyush, Shaurya, Abhijit, Neetu, Anshika and Aarika. My in-laws, Uma Rani Rai and Dr R.K. Rai supported the process of book writing completely. I sincerely appreciate their valuable inputs.

My heartfelt thanks to the legendary Shiv Nadar for his tremendous support and encouragement.

Special thanks to Vineet Nayar and Anant Gupta for their continuous support and inputs on the book.

Thanks you very much to all of my family, friends and colleagues who provided immensely valuable inputs and suggestions. Raju and Meenakshi Ranjan, Prem and Nisha Shukla, Ajay and Madhurani Marathe, Ramesh and Renu Murthy, Jeevak Bhatia and Shikha Gupta, Gangeya Purushottam and Anita Rai, Rahul and Sangeeta Goyal, Vivek and Anjuli Vishwabhan, Raghu Raman Lakshmanan and Revathi Raghuraman, Anoop and Arina Tiwari, Amit and Ruchika Gupta, Anand and Pareezad Birje, Rohit and Misha Bharadwaj, Ajai and Archana Kumar, Vineet and Ruchika Kumar, Rajat, Anuradha and Srijani Ganguly, Vicky and Kanika Gupta, Ashok and Arti Patel, Saurav Adhikari and Madhavi Jha, Amit Varma, Pankaj Bhargava, Kunal Purohit, Krishnan Chatterjee, Anindya Chatterjee, Ajay Davessar, Shantanu Dhar, Vittal Devarajan, Prithvi Shergill, Chau Heather Crawford and Rajat Agarwal.

Thanks to all of my friends and colleagues at HCL and at the IT industry, who have over the years enthusiastically heard me recite my poems on one or the other occasion. I can't thank you enough for your support. Thank you very much for your affection.

I want to extend special thanks to Kapish Mehra, Managing Director, Rupa Publications, for his deep and insightful inputs. Thank you very much to Ritu Vajpeyi-Mohan, Managing Editor, Rupa Publications, for providing the much needed critical help. This book has been published thanks to their untiring help.

Finally and most importantly, the cornerstone of my life—my family. Affectionate big hug and loving thanks to my wife Sushma, daughter Shikha and son Soumya who all helped in reviewing several versions of the draft and provided constant and often critical feedback throughout the writing process. Writing this book took a lot of my time away, which genuinely belonged to them.

Passion for writing is infectious and writing poems, even more. Enormous source of encouragement, affection and love that I have received from all is the only reason I have been able to convert the scattered set of writing into this book of poems.

I hope you enjoyed reading this book, as much as I enjoyed creating it.

Love you all and thanks again.

Cause, Commitment and Support

In India, more than 2 million people migrate from rural areas and small towns to cities in search of a better life every year. In 1951, 17 per cent of the population was urban, and in 2025, it is expectsed to reach 42.5 per cent. Several cities have grown to become megacities and as of 2014, India has four of them: Delhi, Mumbai, Kolkata and Bengaluru. These are cities with a population of more than 10 million people each. India will gain more megacities over the next decade. The lack of market-relevant skills often leads the migrant population to settle for low-paid jobs in these cities.

Only 5 per cent of the 250 million people entering the workforce over the next decade are expected to receive formal vocational training. There is a huge gap between the demand and the availability of young talent. More than 90 per cent of the young population in India works in the informal sector. Youngsters learn on the job without any structured training process. With the growth of urbanization, it is critical to take responsibility for bridging the massive gap between demand and supply through suitable skill development and vocational training programs.

The net proceeds from this book will be donated to the cause of skill development and vocational training programs that will help in bridging this gap.

We have created **Har Asha Foundat**ion, a non-profit organization that provides support to youth in this sector.

Thank you for your kind and generous support.